D0841084

The
Sound
of
Light

Poems

Greg Watson

WHISTLING SHADE
PRESS

Saint Paul, MN
www.whistlingshade.com

First Edition, First Printing

November 2022

ISBN 978-0-9829335-2-7

Book and cover design by Joel Van Valin
Author photo by Neza S.G.

Some of these poems have been previously published in magazines and books, including:

"Perhaps You Were Never So Small" and "In the Newborn Intensive Care Unit" appeared in *The Road by Heart: Poems of Fatherhood* (Nodin Press)

"After the Storm" appeared in *It Starts with Hope: Writings and Images of Hope Donated to the Center for Victims of Torture* (Nodin Press)

"After the Marathon" and "In the Newborn Intensive Care Unit" appeared in *The Saint Paul Almanac*

"It's an Old Story" and "Little Song" appeared in *Whistling Shade*

"These Rooms" appeared in *Boomer Lit Magazine*

"Sauna" appeared in *Kippis!*

"Leaving the Light On" appeared in *The Quiver Review*

"When, For a Moment, I Grow Weary," and "Last Words" appeared in *Autumn Sky Poetry Daily*

Printed in the United States of America

Also by Greg Watson:

Open Door, Open Wall

Annmarie Revisions

Cold Water Memory

Pale Light from a Distant Room

Things You Will Never See Again

The Distance Between Two Hands

What Music Remains

All the World at Once: New and Selected Poems

The Road by Heart: Poems of Fatherhood
(co-edited with Richard Broderick)

In memory of my sister Cherie,
who called me baby brother;
and for Hadley—as always—
who calls me dad.

Contents

One

Two

Three

Storehouse burned down—
Now at last I can see
the moon.

- Mizuta Masahide

One

Perhaps You Were Never So Small

for my daughter

Perhaps you were never as small
as our simple eyes
observed, but merely
coming from a distance
we could not measure,
a star whose light had traveled
centuries before
it could be seen or named.
Perhaps this is the point where
time itself slows
to an audible pulse,
one clenched hand conducting
through the bone-lit dark,
the thick rhythm of
our steps leading
continuously home,
through the shadowless
shift of moon
and vapor trails of memory,
leaning back
into a music that
could only be known by heart,
a music that was somehow
made for us all along,
long before we had bodies
and mouths
with which to sing.

I Have Lived Here All My Life

I have lived here all my life.
Much longer than I could ever recall,
though I try hard to remember
before remembering was possible,
before the framework of faces and forms
emerged to leave and leave again.
Somewhere in that time the stars began
their uncertain meanderings,
memories already to themselves;
somewhere the moon wiped the fingerprints
from its thin, reflecting lens,
down where the river slopes into shadow
and the swaying tangles of trees
lift their wordless prayers,
where the earth itself is a secret
whispered through endless shifting layers.
Some of that light still remains,
flickering in these wet summer grasses,
lingering in my love for you.

After the Storm

There's no silence like the silence
after a storm, the pure and sudden calm
radiating from every saturated leaf
and blade of grass; the slinking, skittish animals
emerging in mute wonder from
the cool shadows of basement rooms.
You remember now, though a lifetime removed,
the lightning flash of your own face
reflected in the window glass, and then gone.
How fleeting the world's violence
seemed in that moment; how fleeting
the fear that arose and flew
from your small, fluttering chest.
Even the thin, silvery moon disappeared,
like a coin from a trickster's hand;
even the stars sank below the surface of night.
There's no silence like the silence
after a storm, no spark or phrase to compare
to the great and noble stillness of a world
reclaimed, if only for a moment,
from a darkness no word could name.
Let it be ours, eternal pulse of the instant,
breathing in, breathing out once again.

End of the Season

A cold mist of stars clings to the rocks,
refusing to rise or be named.

The gray sky recedes to white, clouds
folding themselves into memory;

the rough outlines of freighters
hover in the distance, like a child's

drawing left unfinished.
Now and then someone passes,

shoulders arched stubbornly
against the chilling wind.

All along the shore, docks are taken in,
cars loaded for the long drive home.

Soon the flags will stiffen,
sheets of plastic will be hoisted

to the frames of darkened windows.
And out of nowhere, the half-cry,

half-shriek of a single gull, unseen.
No one would ever think to call it

a song, but it is the last clear
note you may hear until spring.

How Much

There are times I wonder,
in the most ordinary of silences,
how much I had to give up
simply to write the poem that spoke
your name once more—and
how much was lost in the saying.

Three in the Morning

No good news comes at three in the morning. No story ends well from here. No good cheer comes calling, or word of long-held debts forgiven. The sleep-dark stings, and the phone rings like a jar of nails thrown from a high shelf, scattering the shadows in four directions at once. Worst is the knock on the door that cracks like a small ship breaking, waking you with sudden cold. "It's your brother," you hear them say. "There's been an accident." Something small and hidden shatters; something falls, and keeps falling. And, of course, one day there will be news of you as well, though you will be far away, your face and name already a memory dreamed of in such secret hours as these.

Windy Day in Autumn

The autumn wind today shakes
its knotted fists, brings up old grudges,
slaps the tattered flags against
their cold and hollow masts.

One wind climbs the ladder of another.
Crows and finches set out, unsteady
as newborns, blown back into the uncertain
safety of storefront awnings.

Even the clouds appear somehow anxious,
rushing one way, then another,
their thin and tattered layers turned
outward like empty pockets.

Blue and green recycling bins tumble
drunkenly down sidewalks strewn with sand,
from which the simple act of crossing the street
now seems a small, unspoken victory.

But that white spark of a sun has not yet
receded from view, and the first
blinding snow of the season has yet
to dream itself into existence.

We are grateful in our small and secret ways,
grateful even for the grit held between
our teeth, as we move slowly, stubbornly
to whatever still point we can find.

After the Marathon

After the marathon, the runners—surrounded by family, supporters, and strangers—crowd the afternoon trains; bodies exhausted, limbs shocked back into rest, with not-quite-visible wings of steam hovering here and there. Their voices, calm and easy, rise and fall in unassuming waves, punctuated by small peals of laughter. Some still wear their numbers; some draped in silver foil, as if anticipating a burst of celestial weather the rest of us are unprepared for. Dried fruit and nuts are passed from hand to hand, bottles of water glinting in the early October sunlight. For a moment, we are here for this, and only this. We trust the train to carry us forward, trust the day to breathe on our behalf, none of us in any hurry to arrive.

In the Newborn Intensive Care Unit

It is best to speak softly here, to make
only the smallest of conversation with those
in passing; a weary nod in the elevator
is easily understood, acknowledgment of the obvious
and hope for transcendence, however fleeting.
From our cool, windowless room we stand watch,
our tiny daughter breathing in a time signature
we cannot follow, though it surrounds us,
along with our seeming helplessness, learning
what new words and phrases we can—the jargon
of those who know which wire goes where,
which numbers are good news and which
elicit only a slightly somber exhalation.
A gentle and unexpected humor rises between
us, born of a weary necessity. Saltines and tumblers
of chipped ice from the machine down the hall
become an almost religious ritual, as we pass
the small, silent chapel with its huddled
congregation of candles glowing at all hours.
Mostly we wait with the others, sleeping
sporadically on fold-out cots, never sure which
bleeps from the machines signal safety,
and which a possible storm just out of view.

Dream Journal

Perhaps it's time to throw
away those old journals, full of
scribbles and half-finished sketches,
the armchair interpretations
meant to be worked out later,
transcribed as poems,
unaddressed epistles, roadmaps
toward some future clarity.
Perhaps it's time to let
those flickering images spool away
from their slightly dented reels,
to simply close your eyes
and set out walking, ignoring
symbols as you would
a scattering of leaves in the road.
What freedom then, to float
into any room unnoticed,
unencumbered by a lifetime
of nocturnal fear and longing.
When you speak it will be
something marvelously simplistic,
as light as your breathing,
the sliver of a thought you may
or may not choose to reveal.

It's an Old Story

1.

Last night in your sleep, a low humming
sound mingled with your breathing,
like wind moving through hollow reeds
along the lip of an ancient river.
I must have loved you even then,
when I was still mostly rain and cloud
trembling with the weight of gravity,
uncertain where to fall.

2.

It's an old story: the unfathomable wind
stretched thin between the leaves,
cracked eaves and window panes humming
with the turning of the earth;
and here below, two small bodies
folded upon the prayer mat of the bed,
where all our days run suddenly into one
and all we say is spoken by breath.
Nothing more. But nothing less.

Solitude in Autumn

Indelicate clank of the radiator
and the hesitant tapping
of autumn rain. Add one small voice
and you've got a symphony.

You Turned to Leave Like Someone

You turned to leave like someone
who had been practicing
that simple step for years—a dancer
among the unassuming landmarks of
doorways worn by passing hands,
tiny copper bells tied to your ankles
sounding as the violins closed
their windows to the sun.
You have been leaving now
for years, and are not yet gone—
your shadow lengthening
like a river the width of a wrist.
You are leaving even now as
I write these lines in measured haste,
the autumn light dimming
behind black and skeletal trees,
hoping for one more glimpse
of your last and finest act.

Sitting with My Sister

When I received the news today of your
passing—a fact somehow known, viscerally,
before I touched the phone to listen—
I wanted only to keep it to myself,
to not speak to anyone during those
long, slow-moving minutes, their silence
demanding only more silence,
their time, more time. I wanted to hold
you there, secretly, perhaps selfishly,
between that cave of heart and rib cage,
to hold you suspended like a single breath,
or a seed which I was neither able to
swallow or spit out. I wanted to cradle
that moment, inseparable from you,
hovering like a thought not quite formed, not
simply for the sake of sparing others
but to sit with you one last time, as we had
near the end in your tiny apartment,
too quiet for you, and those drugstore
Christmas lights blinking on and off
against the smoky California sun.
I wanted merely to sit with you once more,
just us, before picking up the phone,
handing you back to the world of
the living, the realm you had so recently
left behind, weightless and wordless
now, suddenly beyond the endless
aches and ailments of matter, your absence
only beginning to make itself known.

Visiting My Brother's Grave in Winter

Scarce as leaves, these footprints
among the gray cemetery snow;

small constellations of ice
clinging to my beard.

Moon Angles

Sometimes I wonder what is lost in the naming of things. For my two-year-old daughter, the stars in the night sky are called "moon angles"—as if they were splinters of that greater light turned down upon us, endlessly reflecting. Of course, we must learn what we must learn, to speak of things the way others do. When she is older, I may tell her to forget all of these things, as rivers disappear into mountains and mountains into streams. We can begin where we left off so many years before, speaking softly the first words that arise between us.

Leaving the Light On

Like poetry or painting, the art
of saying goodbye does not
get easier with time or circumstance,
only more familiar.

Your way, it seems, was to say
nothing in a way which no one else
had yet mastered—which
in a brave moment
might be mine as well.

But I am not brave.
I am simply a man constructing
this small house of words
upon a foundation of silence.
The rest I leave to you.

It is not what you might call a home.
Though you, dearly departed,
survive only on wind and sunlight,
the memory of the living.
Your needs are small.

Should you choose to return,
you will find the door has been left
unlocked, the lamp in the living room
still burning a second moon
into the window glass.

There is nothing here worth taking,
nothing we have not already
agreed to lose.

Two

Hymn for a New Year

Let it begin at its own leisure,
somewhere between a sigh
and a shrug, the way the bored
and world-weary signal to each other
on slow-moving elevators,
wordlessly acknowledging their
solidarity through shared uncertainty.
Let this unknowing be our guide,
entering as softly as the first
few hesitant tufts of snow.
Let the wooden temple bells
clack in the wind a moment longer,
their invisible doors unopened
against the bright and knowing sun.
We are lazy students today,
letting the Way find us
for a change, letting all things
find us, however they may, as though
the universe had spun us around
and left us where we fell.

A Winter Postcard

Fresh dunes of snow reach nearly to the window ledge; daggers of ice casting long fence-like shadows along the ground. The wind carves its name into everything. But the woman's voice on public radio speaks only in soothing tones: "There is a wind chill advisory," she coos, as though it were a mild seduction. She implores us all to stay indoors for a day of calm reflection, a day when friends in other parts of the country ask, "Why do you live there?" But there are great poems being written, there are bodies striking the ancient sparks of love, words of comfort and forgiveness that have waited decades to arrive. Survival begins in such small ways—a moment, an hour, a day of quiet persistence. Begins with the gurgle and drip of the coffee pot, someone saying, "Come in, come in, slip out of those wet boots. It seems like ages since we spoke."

Last Words

In the end, I don't need to know what your last words might have been—whether some sly, unassuming wisdom, cry of anguish, or blasphemy—before your body offered up its last and holiest secrets. For you, a man who conserved words as if allotted only a handful in this life, one silence leading into another would seem fitting. The endless books of quotations and insight, the intricate wounds coughed up as speech, we must now leave to others. Even the words I wrote after your death, winding them into a pencil-thin scroll to be fed into cemetery dirt, somehow elude me now. Their mystery is yours, their meaning gone back into darkness. Let it remain so. Let me learn, if anything, the grace of saying nothing at all.

When, for a Moment, I Grow Weary

When, for a moment, I grow weary
from the endless news reports of bombs
dropping from bleak winter skies
and the faceless tanks nudging their way
through streets clogged with rubble,
I turn my mind instead back to that little girl
cradling her ragged doll at her side, there
in the long silence of the subway tunnel
that for tonight has become her bed.
I want to tell her that everything will be alright,
even if that is another bedtime fable,
to sing to her gently in her own language,
as I would to my own child, who sleeps
at this moment in a warm tangle of sheets,
mouth agape, dreaming, I imagine,
of flight, and of saving this broken world.
I have not yet found the perfect words
or melody to make this promise happen,
cannot quite decipher my own voice
through a distance as great as this,
this lullaby merely a litany of questions
turning endlessly back upon itself.
Is the lesson simply that we learn no lessons,
that the old names must soon be worn
smooth to make way for the new?
Still, I continue, offering the only comfort
I can summon, the stubborn light of
one still standing, unable to turn away.

Map

My little girl is learning to draw her world.
Rainbows, ships, bridges, monsters,
and waterfalls—all of them executed
in bold strokes of color—decorate
our walls, floors, and tabletops.
She draws me, her old man, with black stilts
for legs, a small cloud of chin whiskers,
and white balloon of a hand, five-pointed
like the sun, reaching for her own.
In another, the family has merged into
one great being, impossible to tell whose
outstretched arms belong to whom,
or whose feet are leading the way.
But today she gives to me a blank sheet
of paper, folded neatly in quarters.
"This is your map," she says calmly,
"So you will always know where you are."
I accept with the gratitude of the lost.
I treasure this one most of all.

On Being Locked Out of the House

All at once you notice how it goes on without you: the
ceramic owl clock on the end table noting each second; the
endless horizon of books casting their gray, uniform
shadows; the small army of knickknacks, so assured in
their frivolity, their symbolic hominess. One cat sleeps at
the foot of the bed, the other filling out a patch of sunlight
on the rug. You half-expect someone else to walk in and
take your place, perhaps a version of you on a better day.
Of course, this does not happen. But already the late
afternoon light is shifting. Things are moving in slow and
subtle ways. Looking into each separate window, even you
barely notice the absence.

Poem Intended for Two Voices

It's hard to sing with someone
who has a completely different song
in mind. Harder still
to get the silences right.

Mystery Girl

She said her name was
Silence, and to call whenever
I wanted to talk, or even
if I didn't—and sometimes
especially if I didn't. I have been
doing so religiously for all
these years, with little to show
now but these lines written
to and from myself, and to the
nameless gods who hide
amongst the bruised-colored
clouds and answer, in their way,
only when it rains.

Winter Sketches

1.

The sidewalks have all disappeared.
We walk out into blank thought. The hinges
of the mailbox frozen over; the news—
small though it may seem—has traveled
whole lifetimes to reach us.

2.

The wind comes from too many directions
at once, thin white ghosts whirling
across the highway, inventing
themselves at random. We drive for hours
the same stretch of nameless road.

3.

The rooftop below, once slate gray
and clouded with shadow,
becomes with snow a white drawing table
upon which rests the preliminary
sketch of a passing blackbird.

4.

New snow falling on top of the old
this morning. The edges of our world begin
to soften, begin to move closer;
the day rewritten so many times that
no one can say where it began.

It Still Seems Impossible

It still seems impossible, there being
no you—and yet everywhere I look, you
have seemingly just departed.

In every room we knew you have
covered your tracks like a master thief.
You have erased even your words.

What can I speak against such silence?
I turn once more back to winter,
its cold-stiffened list of facts;

I mouth the words on your behalf,
a half-song muffled by the weight of snow,
each syllable a door closing on itself.

The days grow short this time of year,
drag their shadows up by memory.
It is a world made of, and for, absence.

Still, I look for you among the familiar
and unremarkable, nameless places
that you would hardly notice

were you driving through, the roads
themselves all but erased, holiday lights
blinking between the trees.

Scene from a Department Store Parking Lot in Winter

She is saying *No*, as if it were
a mantra; saying *No* to the middle-aged
man, bland but handsome in pea coat
and scarf, his red, chapped hands
pulled from pockets just beginning to fray.
She is saying *No*, though there is no
shouting, no sharp edges to her words.
words that sound merely weary with overuse.
Their breath hangs weightless, separate
in the air between them, drawing
one distance, then another; as he sways
almost indecipherably, turning as if
to leave, turning awkwardly on one heel,
not quite balanced, as though he had
forgotten this simplest of motions.
He feels a sudden stiffness, feels
the cold clutching at his limbs,
as if the size and shape of his body
had somehow offended the air.
She is saying *No*, saying adamantly:
"I cannot go through all of this with you
again." And it may take years before
the good times are remembered
as good once again, and years before
he will hear the calm insistence of
her voice, sending him away, sending him
toward a world and a home he could
only have found on his own.

Used Record Store

You can smell the basements of long ago
here within these cardboard sleeves,
slender spines creased and breaking apart,
can almost feel the dampness seeping through
the cold cinder blocks, stale cigarette smoke
and voices turned suddenly into ghosts.
You can hold the shroud of another world
half-awake, waiting to be rediscovered,
can wander aimlessly the long, narrow aisles
the way you did when you were still a kid,
hungry for any sign of life to find you.
You thought those songs would last forever,
the way summer did in every chorus,
repeated endlessly into a silence not quite.
You thought that girl who taught you
to kiss would stay just a moment longer,
the sound of her laughter like the incantation
of something just beyond your reach.
You are still searching, thumbing the racks
for something you may have missed,
still looking and listening for a message
that has taken so long to find you.

Two Chairs

Two chairs discarded in the alley,
snow-dusted, slumped forward,
waiting for rescue or removal.
Two chairs now empty,
frayed at arms and seams,
abandoned to a swiftly fading past.
Chairs that held perhaps
a man, a woman over meals,
conversation, the soft
and knowing silence of years.
Small seats of comfort
once regal in their simplicity,
familial comfort unspoken
and unknown to others, then or now.
Two modest canvases seen
from a cold angle of sky
that even crows in their cacophony
and haste leave undisturbed.

Keeping Watch

It was not our house, only ours to keep watch over
as your aunt traveled some far land
or other—I forget where—and we spent
the better part of summer young and idle,
making love amongst the smell of dusty wood,
strange perfumes, heavy must when the rains came;
rain and thunder that frightened the cats
and soaked the clothes upon the line.
It was not our home, and it was easier to laugh
at such things, scurrying for candles
when the lights suddenly flickered out,
searching every drawer for a simple kitchen knife,
catching moths the color of antique lamps
and releasing them back into the night.
It was never our house and never ours to leave,
yet when we left, we left for good;
and wherever it stands, I pray it holds a small
pocket of our breathing, voices weighted
with neither anger nor regret, blessing
those who live there now, to live the way
we could only have imagined.

Night Driving

You had argued again, argued yourselves
into opposing corners, neither quite knowing
the reason, or what resolution might
consist of—she storming off to bed, you
staying up, surrounded by the dull throb
of television light, the angular forms
of men and women laughing and embracing
with the ease of well-rehearsed lives.
You stumbled, thoughtless as a shadow
out to the car, crawled the smooth, darkened
streets, names on signs becoming illegible.
You wanted it that way: the slow, measured calm
of forgetfulness, that simple falling away.
Found yourself down by the railroad yards,
the oil tankers and boxcars, mountains
of scrap piled into rust and silence.
A person could leave in any direction,
you remember thinking, wander uncared for
and without care, the way your father did
at fourteen, knowing only motion,
the vague and endless promise of arrival.
But you were neither as reckless nor as brave.
In a moment, you would drive back,
slip into bed with the practiced ease
of a pickpocket, strangely familiar among
the bodies of passing strangers.
You would sleep, and fail to dream.
Decades later, you would still remember
the enormous houses of shadow,
the pencil-gray outline of the steel tracks,
the ghostly sound of a world gone still.

You would remember all of this from a distance,
when it would be too late to change direction,
or to alter your own imperfect script.

These Rooms

Take one last look at these simple
rooms before they crumble
into memory—becoming, as they must,
the unremarkable scenery of a passing show
spoken of to some future lover
or acquaintance; one who will not know
our family's touch or hush of sleep,
our history or language untranslated,
the familial smells that were ours alone.
Rooms that still hold our voices like smoke
clinging to walls and fabric,
handprints like the ghosts of birds ·
trapped in dusty window glass,
rooms the baby first opened her eyes to,
drinking in the good first light of day,
which lingers a moment but never stands still.
Maybe one look is all we are given
in the end, the first and the last merely
reflections mistaken as opposites,
signposts constructed so as not to lose
our way along this shadowed ground, leading
to whatever home will have us now.

Haircut

There was a time when you would
never have let her get this close,
a time when neither of you could be in
the same room for more than a moment.
Her touch was not of your concern,
her words no longer yours to decipher.
But you have no one else to ask
to help with this most ordinary of tasks;
so here you sit, pale and shirtless
in the porcelain chill of bathroom light
as she trims and snips, seemingly
at random, cautiously maneuvering
the electric trimmer across the contours
of your skull, rounding the arches
above your ears, stepping back to consider,
then moving closer, as a lover might
that moment just before a first kiss.
You will not speak of this as an intimacy.
You will manage a simple *Thank you*,
reaching quickly for the worn t-shirt
carelessly tossed upon the radiator,
as if suddenly realizing that you were late
for one appointment or another, or that
something you could not quite name
had startled you into leaving.

Last Photograph with My Sister

I don't know why this photo, the last that
we took together, is muted in grays and sepias,
as if that broad West Coast sunlight was somehow
being filtered through an antique lampshade
or a scrap of newsprint held up to window glass.
You look so small on the bench beside me,
your bird wing shoulders folding in on themselves,
your kind face hovering somewhere between
a smile and a vague sense of surprise.
Your matchstick legs could barely hold you up,
not for long, your balance swimming
in and out like some uncertain dance partner,
seemingly at random. Yet you insisted on
walking with me through Chinatown, buying
a hand-knit sweater and chocolates for your niece,
those red paper lanterns suspended across
every street, as if the streets themselves,
narrow and all but directionless, were merely
an afterthought. You insisted, too, on that
enormous Christmas tree that lit up the wharf,
sea lions barking with hunger, as always,
for all to hear, each blubbery mound and voice
calling out, indecipherable from the next.
We are waiting, in this moment, for one last
taxi to the airport, as ordinary as that.
But the sun was much warmer than it looks,
the palm trees behind us alive and gently swaying,
while the snow back home—three feet of it—
was a few short hours away. I can't blame you
for not missing it, not missing it at all.

I Pleaded with Your Death

I pleaded with your death
as I would with a wayward lover
to come back and reconsider,
knowing our differences
to be great, but holding out
hope like a beggar's cup.
I demanded to take your place
in the land of parentheses
and forgetting; aligned punishment
with survival, and allowed even
simple words to walk six feet
before me. I suppose you
know the rest: the late night calls
that never came, the letters
written in columns of smoke.
Your silence remained steadfast.
It did not shift; it did not utter
a falsehood, not even once.

Three

For Years I Have Sought the Word

For years I have sought the word,
untranslatable in English, that you pressed
against my ear so long ago.
For years it has flickered
on the periphery, a random fleck
of candlewick erasing itself on air,
never close enough to grasp.
More than once I have heard it whispered
in the shuffling of autumn leaves;
more than once I have startled awake
in the cool hum of darkness,
anxious to scribble it in my notebook,
but it lifted from my hand as suddenly as
a bird startled from its shadow.
For years I have sought this word,
untranslatable, that would lead me back
to you, or some version of you
imagined—through every winter of our
silence, every solace left unspoken,
the word I still seek like a sacred stone
to burn away the distance between us,
one word that contains all others:
the one I cannot speak.

Some Poems Refuse

Some poems refuse to let you in.
They put a sign in the window,
let the shop lights go dim.
The whole neighborhood fills with
the echo of their silence.
You must try again tomorrow,
hoping that your stubborn loyalty
may be smiled upon at last.

Sauna

One by one we shuffle in, heel-heavy with work, age, and life. One by one our bodies begin to moisten and glow with heat, steam reaching upward and upward like spirits long forgotten. Sweat rises to the surface and falls, those thin rivers of self we try daily to contain. Bones and muscle and sinew begin to ease. No one speaks of work here, if they speak at all. No one boasts of being anything other. Status, politics, and religion stand outside the door of this sanctuary. What better prayer than this? Weary yet lighter, we ease back into the blue and temperate world, to reclaim whoever and whatever we thought we were only moments before.

Margins

Silence fills the margins of
every book in every corner of the room;

day upon day, year upon year,
its slender, insinuating tide

swelling with each new breath
and lack thereof,

every turning of the yellowed page
and leaf of tarnished bronze.

Judging by such abundance,
the dead have nothing to fear.

We are keeping track of every word
they have not spoken,

recording them as sacred hymns
to be sung in temples

we have constructed on air.

Back in the Day

It's a phrase that gives you away,
a signal that you belong to another time
and place, even if not so far off
in the scheme of things.
It may surprise you as it tumbles
from your lips, ordinary and
unassuming, acknowledgment of
a world that does not cease,
even as something within you has.
Past tense. You hardly notice
your language beginning to shift,
the verbal backward glances.
It's no longer the girl you are looking
for, and definitely not another
version of yourself. You were
hardly there at all, it seems.
Though you had your time, they say.
You had another word for nearly
everything then—a shorthand
between you and all the coming years.
Though you would be hard pressed
to remember any of them now.

Lines for a Last Native Speaker

What becomes of a language
when there is no one left to speak it,
no one to linger over its sighs
and whispers, its sentence-long string
of vowels and secret code
shifting like the sudden weight
of ocean upon the tongue?
What now of those late promises
of love everlasting, the sacred
texts and blasphemies,
the small note slipped discreetly
from one hand to another?
What worth is the word without saying?
Does it fade with the breath
that once carried it with ease,
a ghost returning only to itself,
or to a source unknown?
Does it speak somewhere
outside the realm of the spoken?
Does it leave us anything
but these smooth, blackened pages,
a few etchings in stone,
its pitch of perfect silence
through which we now must mourn?

Whatever Force

Whatever force it was that
brought me to you has slowed
to the stillness of air—barely a breath
audible or felt; so that I remain
all but motionless as you continue
on a course beyond me, leaving
a length of shadow residual as hope,
a hand fluttering across the page
in the lamplight as I write.

Rewrite

Today the gray snow
circles the air with
the weightlessness of dust,
never quite reaching
the ground below.
The bare trees likewise
sketch themselves
with uncertainty, as if
this day were simply
a dress rehearsal.
The birds seem to agree,
having dispatched
only their understudies
to warble through
a few unfinished hymns.
The rest is silence
and waiting, silence
and waiting, the tentative
revision of our own
simple lyric, signed
long before completion,
carried graciously
by the wind.

Face Blindness

Imagine not recognizing the face of the one you love, of passing her by on a gray, wind-swept street in your own neighborhood. Without so much as a pause in your hurried steps. Imagine those fine contours you have cradled in your palms nightly being softened and blurred by some clumsy artist's thumb. Does she stop then to grab you by your half-tucked shirt, shocking you back to love's emphatic embrace; or continue on to break apart like a dream that seemed so vivid only moments before? You would live in fear this way, praying only for release, speaking tentatively, if at all. For if you could not recognize love as earthly and familiar as this, how would you know the face of the divine, saying pardon, slipping quickly behind a storefront of dark, reflecting glass?

Still Gone

If it's true that all we give away
one day returns, it is,
I suspect, only to remind us
that they are still gone—
one mere blink away
from where we left them,
just far enough out of reach
to keep us moving forward,
toward some thin, unwavering light
of no discernible door,
humming that same tired tune,
the words of which we still
somehow manage to get wrong.

For a Character Actor

That was the objective all along, was it not? To slip into the flesh of another, to speak words from a mouth not your own, to become simply *other*? You won the acclaim of peers and audience alike, lined the walls with symbols of your stature; and still, you were able to walk the streets unnoticed. Your look, your age, your accent shifted like the thinning clouds of November. There were times when your own reflection disappointed you, times when someone you met noted that you seemed shorter, or that your eyes were gray instead of blue. Older now, your name begins to escape you, your memories clouded by so many scripted scenes—old friends arriving on cue, great loves that never quite were. Nevertheless, you move forward, toward you know not what. While others study what you created, you are returning bit by bit to a self never fully formed. Like a novice, you are unsure which direction to take. Like a master, you will leave no steps behind you.

Sunday Afternoon at the
Neighborhood Cafe

The elderly couple sitting near the window, here amongst the midday cacophony of voices climbing over voices, coffee cups clanging like broken bells, enjoys their meal in measured silence. You might not notice them at first, this small island of calm, cloud-gray and unassuming, their subtle movements reflected in the glass behind them. They nod, shrug their shoulders in bemused acknowledgement, passing small packets of sugar and thimbles of creamer back and forth, as though they were coded messages. Do not mistake this for nothing. Do not presume they have said all there is to say in this lifetime. They have, it seems, moved beyond the boundaries of words, beyond the Yes and the No, with little need now to comment on what lies plainly here between them.

The Blind Traveler

I cannot undo what I have said
or written years ago, any more than
I can alter its silence with words,
or fill that chasm with an absence
more noble or understanding.

The babbling rain has a lot to say,
but not much of it makes good sense.
Words on the page slant one way,
then another, shifting and fluttering
with the tide of afternoon light.

Consider them, if you must at all,
as poorly constructed maps, their lines
drawn by the hand of a blind traveler,
leading, however circuitously,
to you, and you alone.

Residual

Late into the summer evening
nothing but sunlight
in the tangles of your hair,
the silence between your sighs
settled like dew
upon the windowsill.

Wordless

I wonder if even words of
kindness long for a peace and quiet
outside their borders,
to commune with another
in the calm of a separate solitude,
the way today I long only to be
beside you, our breathing
and bodies entwined
in the wordless amazement
of love and love alone.

How Can I Say

How can I say I love you
when love itself refuses all attempts
at naming and translation?
How to whisper the name of the beloved
without also insinuating my own?
How can I speak only words
when love itself speaks whole kingdoms
built between the fingers
of sleeping hands entwined,
and the breathing of oceans
in our small, silent temple of night?

The Trees

At nine months of age, my daughter's
greatest delight is gazing at the
shimmer and sway of trees
outside the bedroom window.
Each morning she pulls herself up,
taps at the cool glass, laughing
and cooing in a spontaneous
language of wonder. The trees likewise
appear delighted, waving and seeming
to reach outward, offering their
open hands a thousand times over.
She does not question the direction
of the breeze, nor wonder
the name of each variety of tree.
This is unencumbered wisdom, I think.
We are learning our small world
by sight and feel, as patiently
as our hearts will allow.

On Revision

I think of you, Olav Hauge,
relentlessly revising
those distant, early poems
of youth right up until the end,
a hollow-eyed man
wandering the apple orchard
as a chill wind blew in from the sea;
still in search of the music,
still in search of the elusive line.
We are, it seems, constantly
translating ourselves into
a tongue we never learned,
yet can never quite lose.
There was something we meant
to say, something
we should have left out;
the final page always
one of silence, and always
the hardest to master.

Little Song

When you leave
let it be slow and gentle
as the smallest of rains
sweeping across the horizon,
so fine and so subtle
that I hardly notice
the moment when the rain
has ceased to be.

And Learn to Sing Along

The sweetest song I think
I have ever heard is that
of the summer wind,
thick with the tiny clouds
of cottonwood,
pausing between the leaves
as my daughter laughs
in sheer wonder and delight—
the sound of light itself
asking to be recorded,
and no one around to do so
but me, a novice playing
the only way I know,
as my mother did, by ear,
and by feel. Dearest daughter,
if we keep practicing
in this way, I may at last
get it right, these clumsy words
reaching out to the world
and back to you, so that others
too may hear and learn
to sing along.

Made in the USA
Columbia, SC
14 October 2022

69339356R10041